Salzburg Travel G

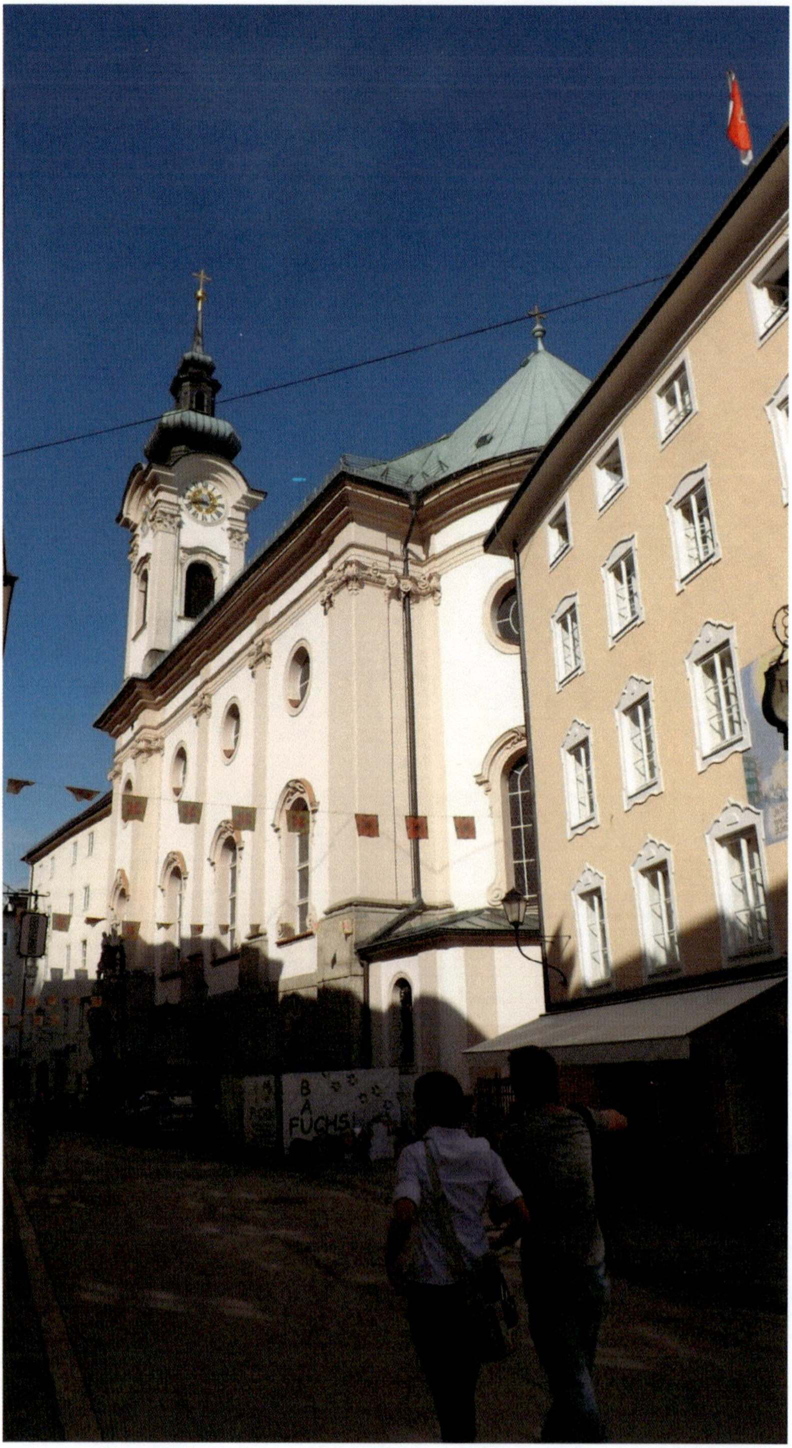
FUCHS!

Table of Contents

Introduction 5
Wolfgang Amadeus Mozart 7
The Weather in Salzburg 9
Important Health Information 10
Recommended Places to Visit in One day 12
The Salzburg Card 13
The Sound of Music 14
    Nonnberg Abbey 15
    Pferdeschwemme or Horse Pond 19
    Residenz Fountain 20
    Mirabell Gardens 22
    Mozart Bridge (Mozartsteg) 25
    Schloss Leopoldskron 27
    Felsenreitschule 30
    The Gazebo, or Pavilion 32
    Mondsee Cathedral 35
    The Sound of Music Bus Tour 38
The Fortress Hohensalzburg 41
    View from Fortress 42
    Festungsbahn 45
Salzburg Cathedral 47
Residence Fountain in Residence Square 51
Horse and Carriage Tour 52
Residence Palace and Salzburg Museum 53
Mozart's Birthplace 54
Gertreidgasse 57
Mirabell Palace 58
Mirabell Gardens 59
Nonnberg Abbey 61
St Peters Abbey 64
Makartsteg Bridge 68

Austrian Food 70

Shopping 75

The Lakes and Mountains 76

Hellbrunn Palace 80

Winter in Salzburg 82

Other Attractions to Visit. 83

    The Salzburg Zoo. 83

    The Salt Mines 83

    Vienna 83

    Keltenblitz 83

    Toboggan runs from the top of the mountain Zinkenkogel in Hallein Bad Duerrnberg. 83

Addresses of Attractions 84

Introduction

If you love historical cities with flair, artistic grandiose buildings, lakes and mountains, then you will fall in love with Salzburg.

The first thing that hits you with Salzburg is its beauty. The buildings are each a work of art in their own right, many have historical significance, centuries old, yet each so different in their design, and all complement each other in complementary shades of pastels. The fortress stands majestically above the city, guarding its jewelled architecture and natural beauty below.

The Salzach River that flows through the city adds to its beauty and charm. You can relax by the river or take a boat ride to view the spectacular scenery.

Salzburg gets its name from the fact it became a rich city due to its salt mines. The salt was mined from the nearby Hallein Salt Mine, also known as Salzbergwerk Dürrnberg and the salt has been mined for over 7000 years, since Stone Age times, now a museum, visitors can experience the salt mine underground, and see how the city gained its riches from the 'white gold.' In 14 BC the Romans invaded the city and built the settlement 'Iuvavum' which is now the site of the Old Town. In the 7th Century Bishop Rupert built St Peters Monastery, and founded the Nonnberg Convent. The Hohensalzburg Fortress began construction in 1077 under the ruling of the Archbishop Gebhard von Helfenstein. It was expanded over the centuries and is now one of the largest medieval castles in Europe.

Salzburg was listed as a UNESCO World Heritage Site in 1997 and is internationally famous for its baroque architecture.

The people of Salzburg are proud of its association with 18th-century composer Wolfgang Amadeus Mozart. He was born in Salzburg and resided there, and as well as visiting these places, now museums, all of the gift shops serve to promote their historical association with Mozart.

Lovers of the movie 'The Sound of Music' will be aware that much of the movie was filmed in Salzburg, and you can trace the footsteps of Maria in the movie and visit some of the settings in the movie. I have included photographs and maps to help you find the locations. Whatever reason you choose to visit Salzburg, you will not be disappointed. It's a beautiful place, steeped in history, nestled between mountains and lakes, a place you will never forget.

They speak the German Language and unless you also speak the language, finding your way through the streets using their German street names can be a little daunting, especially since the streets and squares are not parallel, and I can honestly say I got lost several times and so have included many maps in this book to help you find your destinations, after all I don't want you to waste valuable time on your holiday searching for places like I and many others did.

Wolfgang Amadeus Mozart

Mozart is an important part of Salzburg, and to appreciate Salzburg, you need to appreciate Mozart.

Mozart was born in Salzburg on 17th January 1756 at Number 9 Getreidegasse, which is now a famous street in Salzburg and the house of his birthplace is now a museum. His baptismal records indicate he was named Joannes Chrysostomus Wolfgangus Theophilus Mozart He was the youngest child born to Leopold Mozart and Anna Maria née Pertl, they had seven children but five of them died in infancy, leaving Mozart and his older sister Maria Anna.

His father Leopold was a composer and a teacher and began teaching his elder sister, but on seeing how easily his three year old son began to experiment with the clavier, soon after began teaching him minuets and small pieces, which Mozart played with delicacy and perfect timing. By the age of five he was writing his own music, playing pieces to his father whilst his father recorded his work.

His father soon gave up composing and instead began touring with his two children, playing to Kings and Queens, princes and princesses.

Mozart composed his first opera Apollo et Hyacinthus when he was only eleven years of age.

By the age of seventeen, Mozart was employed as a court musician for the Prince Bishop of Salzburg. His low salary though forced him to travel elsewhere. He travelled to Vienna and Munich and eventually became very successful.

Mozart was known to write music very quickly, he would compose music so he could take it on tour with him to perform; in fact he composed not less than 600 pieces in his lifetime, not matched by any other composer.

In 1781 Mozart proposed to Constanze Weber. They were married at St Stephen's Cathedral in Vienna. They were often separated due to Mozart's travelling career, money was short and he needed to pay the doctors bills. His adoration for his wife is evident in his letters, they both wrote to each other regularly whilst he was away to help keep their love alive. He missed her terribly, and carried her portrait around with him. For the nine short years they were together Constanze was pregnant for much of them, giving birth to six children, where only two survived.

After his marriage Mozart wrote the *Heffner* and *Linz* symphonies and five string quartets. He composed nine piano concertos and three of these concurrently with *The Marriage of Figaro*. He also composed *Eine Kleine Nachtmusik* and the *Clarinet Quintet in A*, three of his 41 symphonies; *Cosí fan Tutte*, three piano trios, *the Coronation* piano concerto, two piano sonatas and three string quartets and the very famous *The Magic Flute*, not long before his death.

He died aged only thirty five years old, in Vienna, in 1791, in the first hour of 5th December two weeks after becoming ill which is believed to have been due to sepsis from an unknown infection.

Mozart is often described as the greatest composer that ever lived. The reason for this is his phenomenal ability to compose so many great masterpieces in such a short life span, not only was he a composer of beautiful symphonies, but also concerto, chamber, choral, instrumental and vocal music, and very gifted at writing opera. He was also not only a composer but was also a conductor, pianist, organist, and violinist.

He was born in Salzburg, and the City of Salzburg celebrate their association with him.

Even if you have not purposefully listened to classical music, you will know some of his works, as his works are often used time and time again in such things as television adverts, movies, cartoons etc.

Probably everyone in today's world has heard Mozart's works. Therefore I believe Salzburg has very good reason to celebrate their association with him and he was very lucky as it was such a beautiful place to be born, grow up and be creative.

The Weather in Salzburg

	Jan	Feb	Mar	April	May	Jun	Jul	Aug	Sep	Oct	Nov	Dec
Average High Temperature °C	4	6	11	14	20	23	25	24	19	15	8	4
Average Low Temperature °C	-4	-2	1	4	9	12	14	14	10	6	0	-3
Average High Temperature °F	39	42	52	57	68	73	77	75	66	59	46	39
Average Low Temperature °F	24	28	33	39	48	53	57	57	50	42	32	26
Average Rainfall in mm	50	50	102	90	115	152	160	163	125	80	84	67
Hours of Sunshine	2	3	4	5	6	6	6	6	5	4	2	1

Due to its geographical location near the mountains, Salzburg does get a lot of rain, even more than the UK. So as long as you are prepared for rain you should cope with it better, therefore a brolly and a light Mac should be on your list of essentials to take with you in the summer, and winter clothing, gloves, hats and boots in the winter.

I went in July, and I did come home with a tan, it did rain half of the time I was there, but the rest of the time it was blazon sunshine and at least 26°C. The drains coped really well with the rain, and even after a downpour, the water disappeared as soon as it came.

From November fog, rain and snow is common.

Important Health Information

Although Austria does have mosquitoes they do not carry Malaria.

TICK ALERT

Tick Borne Encephalitis is endemic in all of Austria's federal states. TBE is carried by rodents, and passed onto the ticks feeding on the rodents, which in turn pass it onto humans after latching onto the skin. Some of the woodland surrounding the lakes some of the forests and even some parks have ticks carrying the disease. The undergrowth near the roadsides may also be prevalent. These ticks can carry the bug 'Tick Borne Encephalitis' which can cause severe illness. The virus causes similar symptoms to meningitis. You can read more about the disease here:

http://www.tickalert.org and

http://www.tbe-info.com/upload/medialibrary/Monograph_TBE.pdf

For media and general enquiries call +44(0)1943468010 or email info@tickalert.org

Please follow the information given on the internet sites linked above but generally the disease has commonly a seven to fourteen day incubation period or it could be longer up to 28 days then the first stage consists of flu like symptoms with a high temperature which lasts less than a week usually, followed by a period of feeling normal for a week or two. An unlucky third of those affected may go on to develop the second stage which consists of symptoms similar to meningitis, that is high fever, headache, nausea and vomiting and then more severe symptoms of encephalitis which may affect speech and consciousness and also the facial nerves and mental health. The disease can escalate and cause death so should be taken seriously.

The City of Salzburg itself is said to be a safe area, as the riskier areas are the woodlands. It pays to do research before you go. If you will be participating in outdoor activities, it is recommended that you wear light coloured clothing with long sleeves, and long trousers, tucking your trousers into your socks and inspecting your clothes and skin daily to see if you can find any ticks. Ticks generally will find a place where it may be undisturbed such as the groins, armpits and under breasts.

If you find a tick on your skin they recommend removing it with tweezers, putting them close to the skin and pulling without twisting. Then remove any bits left over. It may be that you don't have tweezers in that case they recommend using some thick tissue and to cover the insect, then pull it off without jerking or twisting. Even if you manage to get it off there is no guarantee you will be risk free from the disease. Around 10% of ticks in those areas carry the disease.

There is a vaccination available; FSME-IMMUN, if you live in the UK you will need to pay for this privately via your GP. People from other countries should check with their own doctors how to get the vaccination. You should really have the vaccination at least a month before travelling but please check with your doctor, or ring the number listed above for further details about the disease or vaccinations.

The TBE vaccination is recommended for:

- Those travelling to warm forested parts of the endemic areas, particularly in the spring and summer, where ticks are most prevalent.
- Individuals, who hike, camp, hunt and undertake fieldwork in endemic forested areas.
- Those who will be going to reside in an area where TBE is endemic or epidemic, particularly those working in forestry, woodcutting, farming and the military.

You should also be aware that the disease can also be passed on from raw milk from goats, sheep or cows. But this is rare.

Emergency telephone numbers in Salzburg:

Ambulance 144

Fire 122

Police 133

Euro- Emergency 112

Medical emergency 141

You will be able to drink the water from the tap and it is premium quality.

Recommended Places to Visit in One day

Of course without knowing your interests and the reason why you would like to visit Salzburg or how long you will be staying I can give a few recommendations of places to visit if time is short.

The best thing to do is head for the city centre which is fairly compact, and you can explore the city on foot very easily.

My top five places to visit in Salzburg are:

1. The Fortress Hohensalzburg. The scenes from the top are breathtaking and please don't go without your camera, you will get some amazing shots of the beautiful city below.
2. Getreidegasse. This popular busy street consists of buildings from the 13th to 16th century and has a character all of its own. It also houses the famous birthplace of Mozart at No 9.
3. Mirabell Garten (Mirabell Gardens) not only is it a reminder of the movie 'The Sound of Music' but it is the gardens of a stately palace and a beautiful place to explore and unwind.
4. Makartsteg bridge, (The Lover's Bridge) Covered with padlocks from lovers declaring their devotion to each other. Decorate a padlock and take it with you, then throw the key away.
5. Mozart's Birthplace. It has three floors of important historical content to explore, including the instruments he played and even documents he has written.

Of course as the purpose of this book is to help you get the most from your holiday I will go into more detail about the best places to visit later in the book. This section is for those visiting with limited time to explore. The addresses can be found in the back of the book.

The Salzburg Card

The Salzburg Card is a card you pay for in advance that allows you into paying venues such as museums for free. More information about the Salzburg Card can be found here
http://www.salzburg.info/en/sights/salzburg_card

You can use the card on the public transport, and get discounts for theatre and concerts too.

But you need to know that the card is limited for the set period you buy it for. I bought a daily card on my first day, and spent the day exploring and looking for places, and got lost more than once, so I didn't get the full value I paid for the card. So it takes planning. Some of the places you might want to visit are free, some you need to pay for, and so you may not actually need the card. It also puts pressure on you to visit as many places you can in a day to get your value, and may then not give every place its due attention.

So please look it up on line and read the small print.

They can be bought in most hotels, so you shouldn't have a problem finding them. There are also kiosks that sell them and shops. But you can buy them online too.

In 2014 the price for an adult for one day in summer is 26 Euros and 36 Euros for a three day card.

The Sound of Music

Maria pictured outside Nonnberg Abbey. Picture Courtesy of 20th Century-Fox Film Corporation

The much loved movie of 'The Sound of Music' was shot in various locations around Salzburg, so I recommend you watching the movie before your visit as the locations are very similar to what they were in the 1960s when the movie was made.

The movie is based on a true story about a nun from the abbey who married a captain with many children. But the locals are protective of their famous nun, and will tell you a tale of how she wasn't paid any money for her story and how the plot in the story differs from her own life. In fact do not be surprised if the locals have not even seen the movie. They may be perplexed therefore to see 'The Sound of Music' touring buses pass them by, or see memorabilia on sale in gift shops. The original Von Trapp mansion is a hotel today but not as glamorous as the lakeside mansion used in the movie.

The Sound of Music lovers though may be a little disappointed in that Mozart is seen as the real hero of Salzburg, and you will notice the difference in gift shops and may struggle to find The Sound of Music memorabilia. But at least you can be heartened that you can walk in the footsteps of Julie Andrews and co and witness such breath taking beauty of Salzburg for yourself.

I advise you to look at the following photographs of the locations carefully before you go. I made the mistake of going to Salzburg thinking all of the locations would be highlighted and would be easy to find, but then was disappointed when they weren't. It was only after returning that I was able to sift through my photographs and watching the movie again did I realise I had indeed been at the exact locations in the movie. I remember wandering around looking for the Abbey, and met others who too were also wondering which building it was, so these photographs are there to help you, to take with you before you go, so you can be happy you are visiting the exact locations in the movie. I would also recommend you sit with this book on your lap as you watch the movie again, make it a game, spot the location, good for kids to play too. Most of the locations are tourist attractions in their own right and will cover these attractions in more detail later in the book.

Nonnberg Abbey

Above – The Nonnberg Abbey today.

This Abbey is where Maria lived and worked, and it is the site where the children visited looking for her after she left. It is also the site where Maria came out, on her way to the Captain's house for the first time, and singing 'No Confidence'. Comparing the movie location hardly, anything has changed. If you walk through the small archway at the top on the left you will see some stunning views of the mountains. See photograph below.

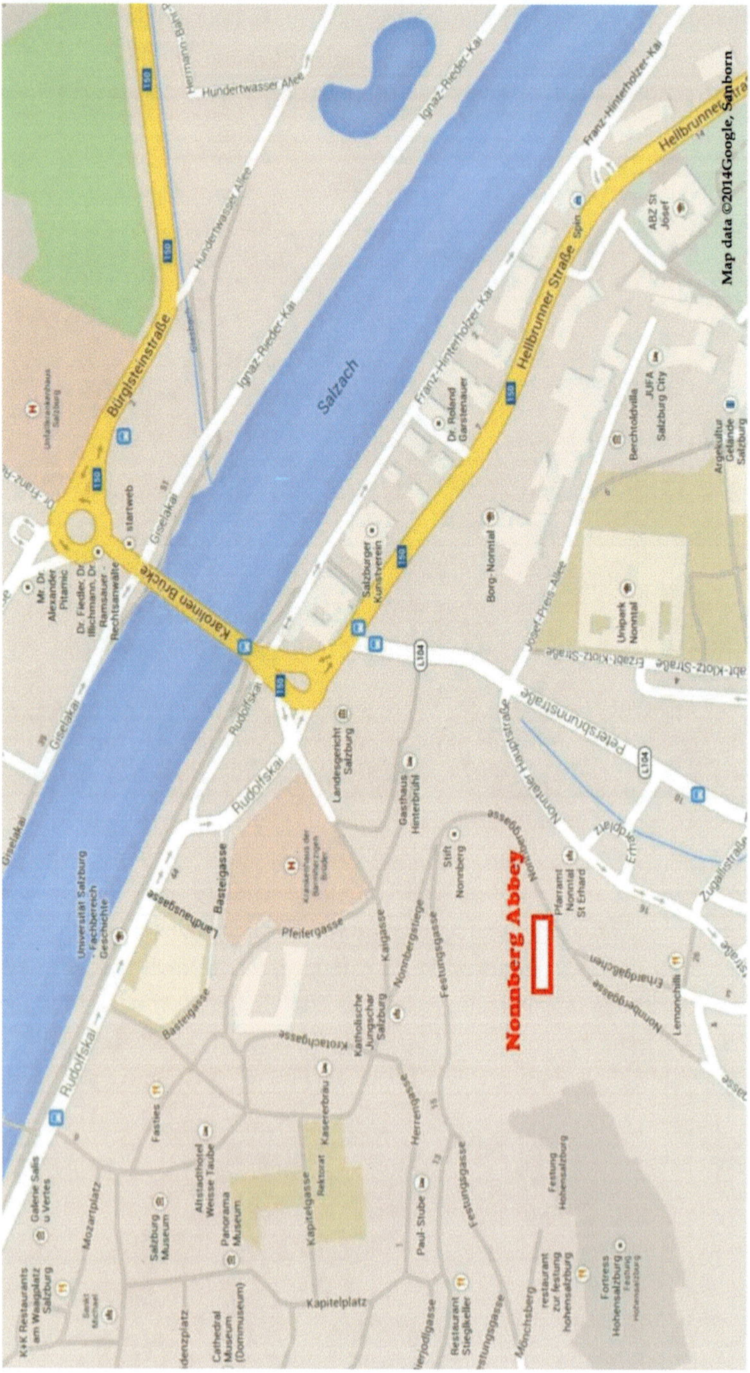

Map data ©2014Google, Sanborn
Nonnberg Abbey
Salzach
Bürglsteinstraße
Karolinen Brücke
Giselakai
Rudolfskai
Ignaz-Rieder-Kai
Franz-Hinterholzer-Kai
Hellbrunner Straße
Hundertwasser Allee
Petersbrunnstraße
Nonntaler Hauptstraße
Josef-Preis-Allee
Erzabt-Klotz-Straße
Erhardplatz
Zugallistraße
Nonnberggasse
Erhardgäßchen
Nonnbergstiege
Festungsgasse
Kaigasse
Pfeifergasse
Basteigasse
Krotachgasse
Herrengasse
Kapitelgasse
Kapitelplatz
Mozartplatz
Mönchsberg
Stift Nonnberg
Pfarramt Nonntal St Erhard
Landesgericht Salzburg
Gasthaus Hinterbrühl
Salzburger Kunstverein
Borg- Nonntal
Unipark Nonntal
Berchtoldvilla
JUFA Salzburg City
ABZ St Josef
Dr. Roland Garstenauer
Universität Salzburg - Fachbereich Geschichte
Katholische Jungschar Salzburg
Kasererbräu
Fasties
Altstadthotel Weisse Taube
Salzburg Museum
Panorama Museum
Paul- Stube
Restaurant Stieglkeller
restaurant zur festung hohensalzburg
Festung Hohensalzburg
Fortress Hohensalzburg
Cathedral Museum (Dommuseum)
K+K Restaurants am Waagplatz Salzburg
Galerie Salis u Vertes
Lemonchilli
Mr. Dr. Alexander Pitamic
startweb

The entrance to the Abbey that was used in the movie. This is in fact the entrance to the church, that you can explore, but the Abbey itself is out of bounds.

This is the doorway of the church where Maria exited with her suitcase and guitar in hand before her journey to meet the captain and the children for the first time.

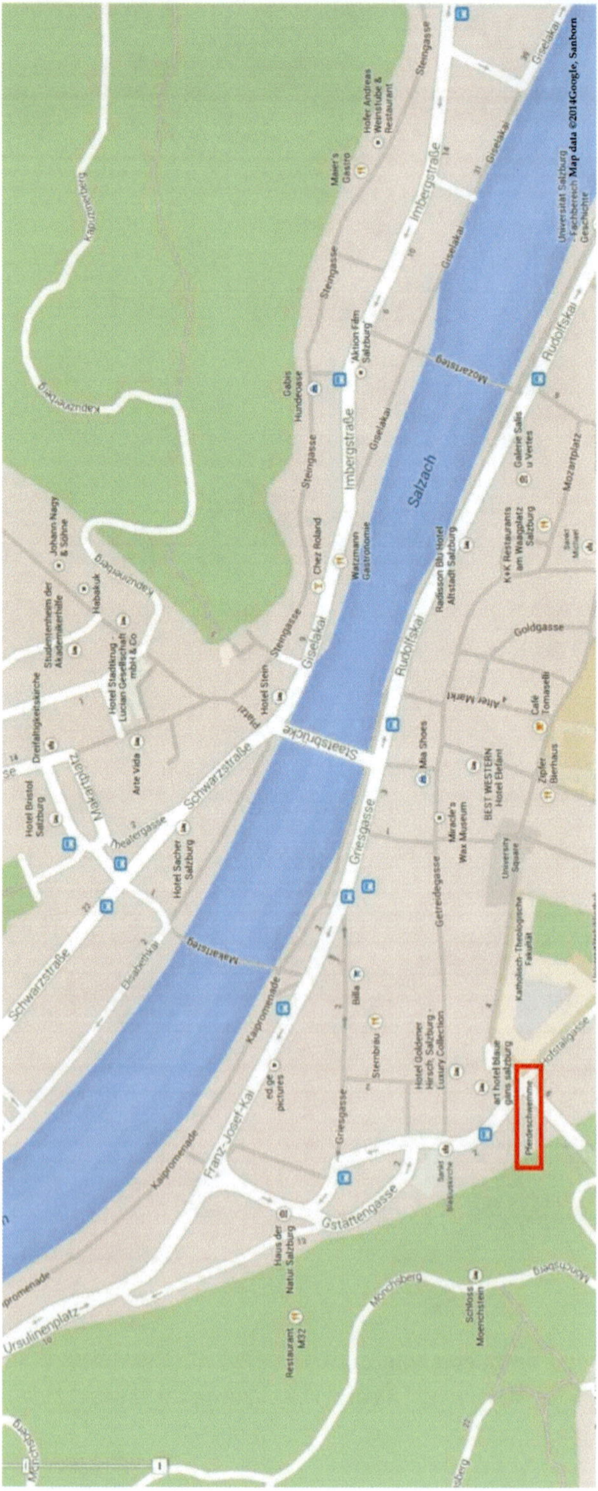
Map data ©2014Google, Sanborn
Salzach
Giselakai
Imbergstraße
Steingasse
Rudolfskai
Mozartsteg
Staatsbrücke
Makartsteg
Schwarzstraße
Makartplatz
Theatergasse
Elisabethkai
Griesgasse
Franz-Josef-Kai
Kaipromenade
Gstättengasse
Getreidegasse
Goldgasse
Mozartplatz
Kapuzinerberg
Mönchsberg
Ursulinenplatz
Pferdeschwemme

Pferdeschwemme or Horse Pond

Maria and the children pass The Horse Pond on their way to their picnic. It is almost identical to as it was fifty years ago.

Pferdeschwemme (Horse Pond)

Residenz Fountain

Residence Fountain is used in the setting in the movie as Maria; Julie Andrews sang 'No Confidence' as she passes Salzburg Museum then makes her way through the square on her way to the Captain's house. She flicks the water in the fountain.

21

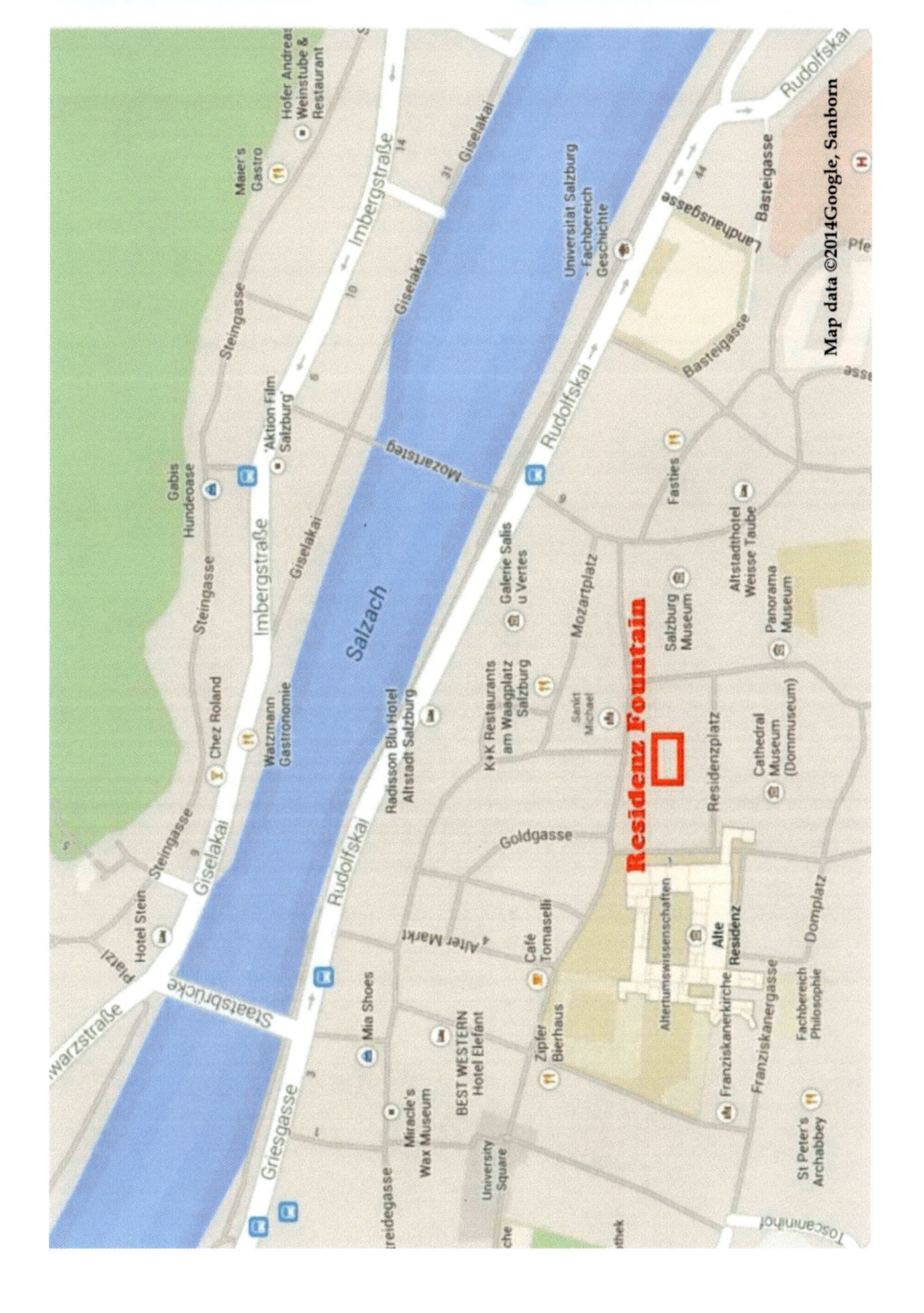

Mirabell Gardens

The movie uses many shots from Mirabell Gardens.

Below Pegasus Fountain in Mirabell Gardens. The children skip around the fountain singing the famous 'Do- re- mi'

Mirabell Gardens
Map data ©2014Google, Sanborn
Mirabellplatz
Mirabell Palace
Salzach
Elisabethkai
Müllner Hauptstraße
Mönchsberg
Kapuzinerberg
Giselakai
Imbergstraße
Rudolfskai
Franz-Josef-Kai
Getreidegasse
Salzburg Cathedral
Salzburger Festspielhaus
St Peter's Archabbey
Paris-Lodron-Straße
Schrannengasse
Bergstraße
Hotel Sacher Salzburg
Haus der Natur Salzburg
Die Stadtalm
Hotel Neutor
Neutorstraße
Reichenhaller Straße
Doktor-Ludwig-Pr
St Sebastian's Cemetery
Hotel Mozart
Hotel NH Salzburg City
Hotel Hofwirt BetriebsgmbH
Maier's Gastro
Arte Vida
University Square
Salzburg Museum
Altstadthotel Weisse Taube
Bärenwirt
Pfarramt Mülln
Heiliger Markus

Maria and the children run through this archway during their song in the movie.

Above is the backdrop for the famous Do re mi song. Maria and the children use the steps as scales during the song.

Mozart Bridge (Mozartsteg)

Maria and the children run across the bridge on their way to their picnic.

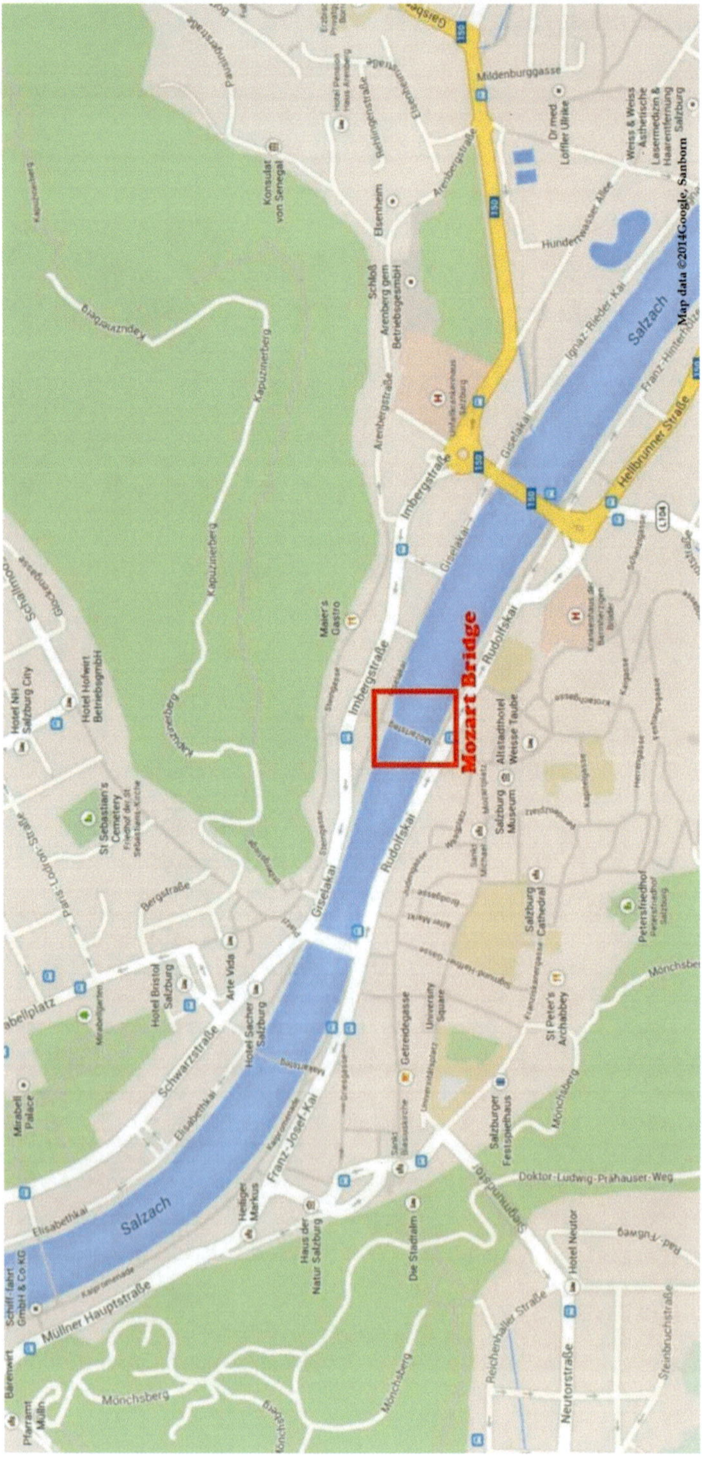
Mozart Bridge
Map data ©2014Google, Sanborn
Salzach
Imbergstraße
Rudolfskai
Giselakai
Franz-Josef-Kai
Elisabethkai
Schwarzstraße
Kapuzinerberg
Mönchsberg
Müllner Hauptstraße
Hellbrunner Straße
Ignaz-Rieder-Kai
Salzburg Cathedral
University Square
Getreidegasse
Mozartsteg

Schloss Leopoldskron

Some will tell you that the terrace at the palace was used for many of the scenes in the movie. It was in fact the adjacent building they used but copied and built the horse guards on the gate and part of the terrace to make it look like the palace. It was here the children and Maria fell in the lake, Maria had an argument with the captain, and where the children played ball with the Baroness Schraeder before finding out she was going to become their mother. I got lost walking trying to find my way to this location and gave up, but 'The Sound of Music Tour, actually takes you to the lake where you can take photographs of the back side of the palace and its terrace. You will need a zoom camera though if you want to capture the horse guard terrace of Schloss Leopoldskron. I believe the building is now a hotel.

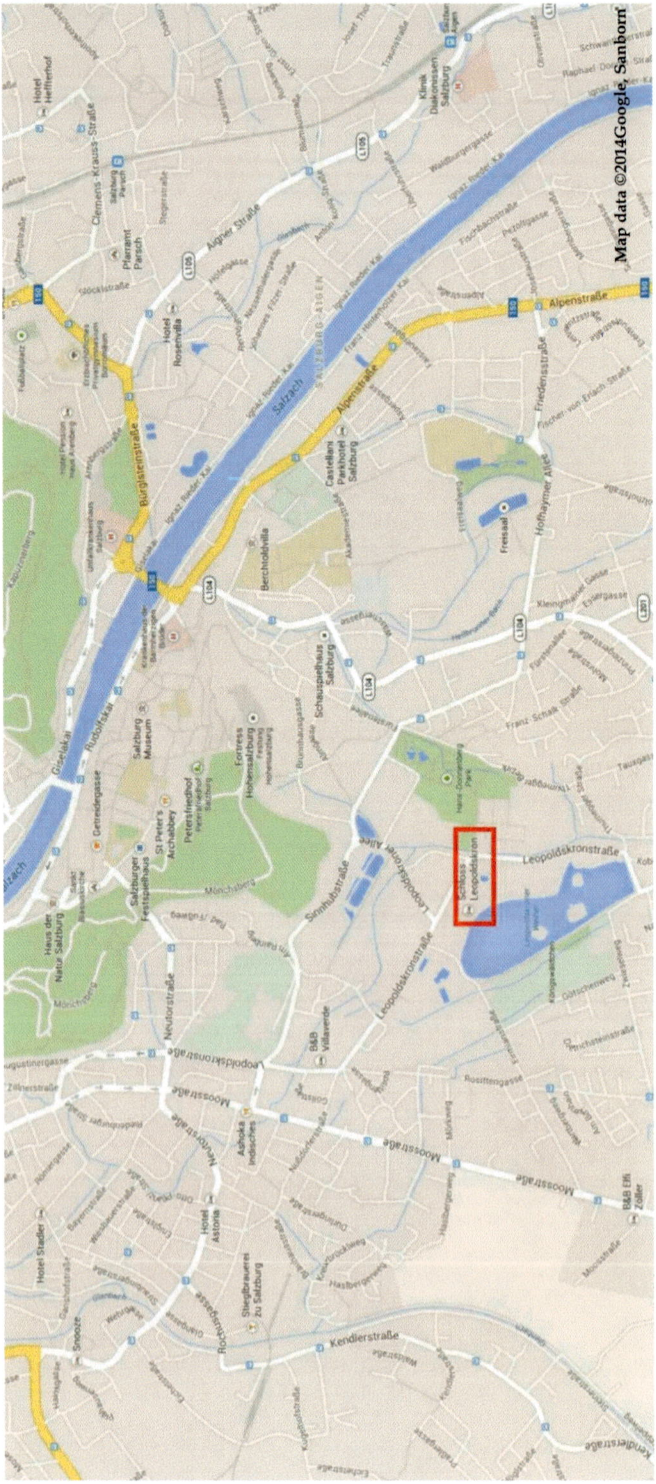
Map data ©2014Google, Sanborn
Salzach
Alpenstraße
Leopoldskronstraße
Moosstraße
Kendlerstraße
Neutorstraße
Schloss Leopoldskron
Fortress Hohensalzburg
Salzburg Museum
Petersfriedhof
St Peter's Archabbey
Salzburger Festspielhaus
Getreidegasse
Haus der Natur Salzburg
Rudolfskai
Giselakai
Bürglsteinstraße
Aigner Straße
Hotel Rosenvilla
Castellani Parkhotel Salzburg
Berchtoldvilla
Schauspielhaus Salzburg
Freisaal
Hofhaymer Allee
Friedensstraße
Hans-Donnenberg Park
Sinnhubstraße
Leopoldskroner Allee
B&B Villaverde
Ashoka Indisches
Hotel Astoria
Stieglbrauerei zu Salzburg
Rochusgasse
Hotel Stadler
Snooze
B&B Elfi Zoller
Klinik Diakonissen Salzburg
Hotel Helffterhof
Clemens-Krauss-Straße
Pfarrant Parsch
Mönchsberg

The terrace at Schloss Leopoldskron.

Below, the front of the mansion in the movie, when Maria first enters the gates of the Mansion is the rear of the Schloss Frohnburg, Frohnburg Palace.

Felsenreitschule

Felsenreitschule is the theatre where the Von Trapp Family performed their farewell song and then escaped.

The theatre is photographed here on the right.

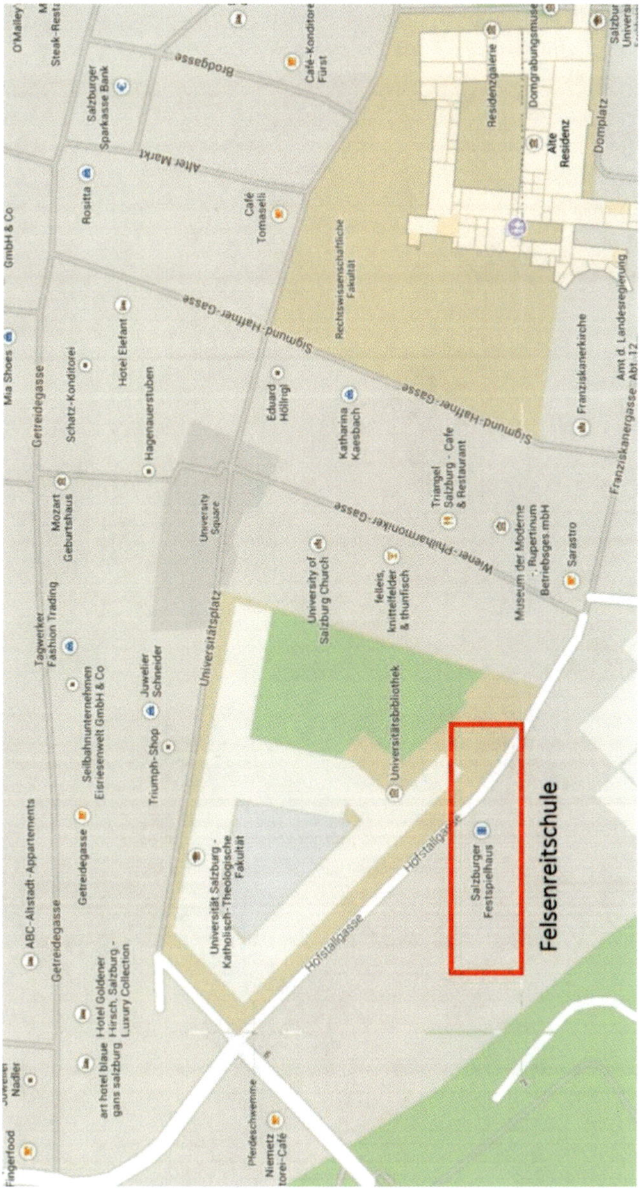
Felsenreitschule
Salzburger Festspielhaus
Hofstallgasse
Universitätsbibliothek
Universität Salzburg - Katholisch-Theologische Fakultät
Universitätsplatz
University Square
University of Salzburg Church
Wiener-Philharmoniker-Gasse
Sigmund-Haffner-Gasse
Rechtswissenschaftliche Fakultät
Museum der Moderne - Rupertinum Betriebsges mbH
Sarastro
Triangel Salzburg - Cafe & Restaurant
Franziskanerkirche
Franziskanergasse
Amt d. Landesregierung Abt. 12
Alte Residenz
Residenzgalerie
Domplatz
Getreidegasse
Mozart Geburtshaus
Hagenauerstuben
Hotel Elefant
Café Tomaselli
Alter Markt
Brodgasse
Café-Konditorei Fürst
Salzburger Sparkasse Bank
Rosittta
Schatz-Konditorei
Eduard Höllrigl
Katharina Kaesbach
Tagwerker Fashion Trading
Seilbahnunternehmen Eisriesenwelt GmbH & Co
Juwelier Schneider
Triumph-Shop
ABC-Altstadt-Appartements
Hotel Goldener Hirsch, Salzburg - Luxury Collection
art hotel blaue gans salzburg
Pferdeschwemme
Mia Shoes

The Gazebo, or Pavilion

The Gazebo used for the famous 'I am sixteen going on seventeen' song.

The Gazebo was moved so that visitors can have easy access to it, but unfortunately you cannot go inside as they had reported many injuries with tourists trying to dance along the benches like the stars in the movie. There was a larger version created in the studio for the filming of the dancing. The Gazebo is positioned in the Hellbrunn Palace gardens and 'The Sound of Music Tour' actually takes you there. It may be difficult to find on your own but I have included the map above and all addresses are in the back of the book if you decide to make your own way there.

Albus Bus Company is still going today and have some old similar styles buses in service. The bus below was photographed near the Gazebo at Hellbrunn Palace. Albus Bus Company still runs similar style buses today with the same location point as a drop off

Maria gets off the bus on her journey to the Captains house.

Picture Courtesy of 20th Century-Fox Film Corporation

Gazebo
Sound of Music Pavilion
Map data ©2014Google, Sanborn
Salzach
Alpenstraße
Hellbrunner Straße
Hellbrunner Allee
Fürstenweg
Schloss Hellbrunn
Hellbrunn-Lustschloss zu Salzburg
Morzger Straße
Montforterweg
Lasserhofweg
Emsburg
Emslieb
Blienhofweg
Der Bäcker Ketter
Postamt Morzg
Gasthof Rechenwirt
Bau- Konform Gesellschaft Mbh
Mayer & Co Beschläge
Porsche
Avanti
Alexander-Moissi-Straße
Karl-Emminger-Straße
Salzachweg
Klausbachweg
Austraße
Floßerweg
Eschenweg
Holzbachweg
Lindenweg
Postbriefkasten
Gärtnerweg
Paß Lueg-Straße
General-Albori-Straße
Glasenbach
Stegweg
Kinostraße
Johann-Herbst-Straße
Kandlweberweg
Militärbachstraße
Kasernenstraße
Tourismusverband
Rainer Kaserne (Militärkirche)
Salzburger Studentenwerk Franz v. Sales Kolleg
PERRO
Kreuzhofweg
Hellbrunner Bach
Treppelweg

Mondsee Cathedral

Mondsee Cathedral is the setting in the movie of Maria and the Captain's wedding. It's around 27km from Salzburg, around a twenty minute car journey. The 'Sound of Music Tour' drops you off in Mondsee and allows you some time to explore. But if you are able to hire a car, there is some very beautiful lakes and scenery in the area, a must see location.

Mondsee Cathedral

Mondsee
Salzburg
Freilassing
Hallein
Bad Reichenhall
Seekirchen am Wallersee
Henndorf am Wallersee
Eugendorf
Thalgau
Fuschl
St Gilgen
St. Wolfgang im Salzkammergut
Strobl
Unterach am Attersee
Innerschwand
Sankt Lorenz
Zell am Moos
Tiefgraben
Oberwang
Enzersberg
Plainfeld
Hof bei Salzburg
Koppl
Ebenau
Faistenau
Hintersee
Krispl
Adnet
Bad Vigaun
Oberalm
Puch bei Hallein
Elsbethen
Anif
Grödig
St. Leonhard
Glanegg
Marktschellenberg
Wals
Bergheim
Anthering
Elixhausen
Hallwang
Kalham
Schwaighofen
Egg
Abersee
Saaldorf-Surheim
Surheim
Ainring
Piding
Pidingerau
Aufham
Winkl-Landthal
Bischofswiesen
Austria
Germany
Map data ©2014 Google, Sanborn

The Sound of Music Bus Tour

There are other bus companies that do the Sound of Music tour, but I can only tell you about the company I went with and that was with the same bus company that ferried Maria to the Captain's house Albus.

You can find details of the tour at www.salzburg-sightseeingtours.at

You can call them on +43662881616 and email them on info@salzburg-sightseeingtours.at. Their departure and drop of point is at sightseeing tours Mirabell Platz 2 A-5020 Salzburg.

It is best to book online before your holiday, so you will not be disappointed. They even arrange to pick you up from your hotel by courier service all included in the price. They drop you off at their terminal which is adjacent to Mirabell Gardens and you can also join the tour from here, and there is also a booth where you can book tickets. They also do other tours such as a tour of the lakes and the salt mines. More details can be found on their website.

Our guide was a very charming man from Spain, and throughout the tour he kept us informed about the buildings and geographical features in the movie.

We were though not taken to sites within Salzburg city centre including those in Mirabell Gardens or the Abbey, but these were pointed out to us. As the tour was to go out of town to the Gazebo and to Mondsee they needed to prioritise with the time allowed.

In 2014 the price is around 35 Euros each, and there is a morning tour and an afternoon tour but please check their website for current details.

I went on the morning tour; I was picked up from my hotel at 9am, then taken to the departure point on Mirabell Platz then and dropped off here at around 1.30 pm.

I thoroughly enjoyed my trip and would recommend it to anyone whether you are a fan of the Sound of Music or not. The guide was really friendly and informative and told me other things about the movie I did not know.

A trip you will enjoy and remember.

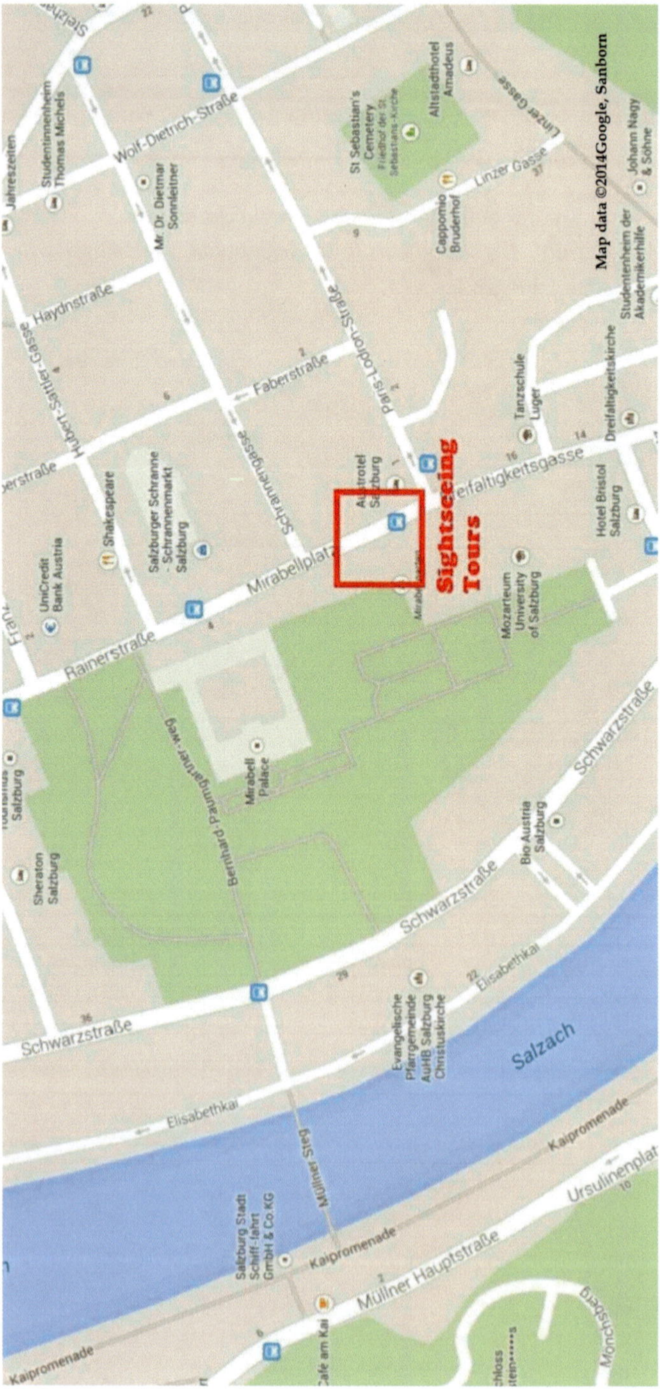
Sightseeing Tours
Map data ©2014Google, Sanborn
Mirabellplatz
Rainerstraße
Schwarzstraße
Elisabethkai
Kaipromenade
Müllner Hauptstraße
Müllner Steg
Salzach
Wolf-Dietrich-Straße
Haydnstraße
Faberstraße
Paris-Lodron-Straße
Dreifaltigkeitsgasse
Linzer Gasse
Hubert-Sattler-Gasse
Schrannengasse
Bernhard-Paumgartner-Weg
Mirabell Palace
Mozarteum University of Salzburg
Austrotel Salzburg
St Sebastian's Cemetery
Altstadthotel Amadeus
Sheraton Salzburg
Hotel Bristol Salzburg
Dreifaltigkeitskirche
Bio Austria Salzburg
Evangelische Pfarrgemeinde AuHB Salzburg Christuskirche
Salzburg Stadt Schiff-fahrt GmbH & Co.KG
Ursulinenplatz
Mönchsberg
UniCredit Bank Austria
Shakespeare
Salzburger Schranne - Schrannenmarkt Salzburg
Cappomio Bruderhof
Tanzschule Luger
Cafe am Kai

The Fortress Hohensalzburg

The Fortress is the first thing you will notice as you enter Salzburg City. It stands majestically on the Festungsberg mountain top towering above and protecting the whole city. It is claimed to be the largest Fortress in Europe. Its foundations were laid in 1077 under the ruling of Arch Bishop Gebhard, and was continually being enlarged until the 17th century. It is fortified with towers, bastions and entrenchments and can claim it was never captured. The only time it actually came under attack was in 1525 during the German Peasant's War when the townsfolk tried to oust Prince-Archbishop Matthäus Lang, but were not able to seize the castle. The fortress though was surrendered without a fight to the French troupes during the Napoleonic War in 1800. It was used as a barracks, storage depot and dungeon but was later abandoned in 1861. It became a tourist attraction around 1892. Later it was used to house prisoners of war from World War one, and later became part of the German Anschluss in the 1930s when Germany occupied Austria.

Inside you will find museums including a puppet museum and one housing armour and artefacts from Salzburg's history but the view from the fortress is absolutely spectacular, and well worth the visit and trip in the shuttle train.

View from Fortress

Above, view of the Fortress from the rear. Below, an aerial view of the fortress.

One stunning room to explore is 'The Golden Chamber'; its walls are ornately decorated with blue tiles and motives and in one corner stands 'The Majolica Stove' an ancient furnace dating back to 1501. It is beautifully decorated with religious scenes, flowers and fruits.

Above one of the displays in the Marionette Museum inside the Fortress.

Festungsbahn

The shuttle train the Festungsbahn shuttles passengers to the top and has been running since 1892. It takes only a minute to shuttle its passengers to the top, and carries over a million passengers each year. You can find it on the street of Festungsgasse. Behind the Salzburg Cathedral.

Map data ©2014 Google, Sanborn
Karolinen Brücke
Giselakai
Rudolfskai
Rudolfskai
Kajetanerplatz
Kajetanerplatz
Landesgericht Salzburg
Bezirksgericht Salzburg
Petersbrunnstraße
Salzburger Kunstverein
Gasthaus Hinterbrühl
Krankenhaus der Barmherzigen Brüder
Basteigasse
Landhausgasse
Pfeifergasse
Kaigasse
Nonnbergstiege
Festungsgasse
Stift Nonnberg
UTILO
Bobs Special Tours
Krotachgasse
Kasererbräu
Pfeifergasse
Kaigasse
Altstadthotel Weisse Taube
Salzburg Museum
Mozartplatz
Kapitelgasse
Rektorat
Herrengasse
Restaurant Stieglkeller
Bierjodlgasse
Festungsgasse
Festungsbahn
Petersfriedhof
Kapitelplatz
Salzburg University
Residenzplatz
Residenzgalerie
Alte Residenz
Mozartplatz
Goldene Ente
Café Tomaselli
Stiftskirche Sankt Peter
St. Peter Stiftskeller
Mönchsberg

Salzburg Cathedral

The Salzburg Cathedral dates back to the 8th century. The first dome was erected by Abbot Bishop Virgil during 767-774 AD. The cathedral was later consecrated to St. Virgil and St. Rupert. It has altered during the years and after a fire in 1568 was completely rebuilt. Today's cathedral was designed by an Italian court architect Santino Solari in 1614 under Archbishop Markus Sittikus. However during the Second World War the cathedral was damaged by bombs in 1944, and was restored in 1959.

The entrance from Domplatz will give you access to the cathedral. On entering look carefully at the three enormous heavy bronze doors, they are decorated with the symbols from left to right, Faith, Love and Hope.

The interior is magnificent and also houses the baptistery where Mozart was baptised and not to be missed. .

The Four statues in front of the entrance are the apostle Peter and Paul and the patron saints Rupert and Virgil.

On entering the cathedral you will see it has the wow factor. Mainly for many beautiful paintings that decorate the interior. Above the archways on either side of the church the paintings depict the fourteen Stations of the Cross.

The ceilings inside the cathedral are an important feature and are amazing.

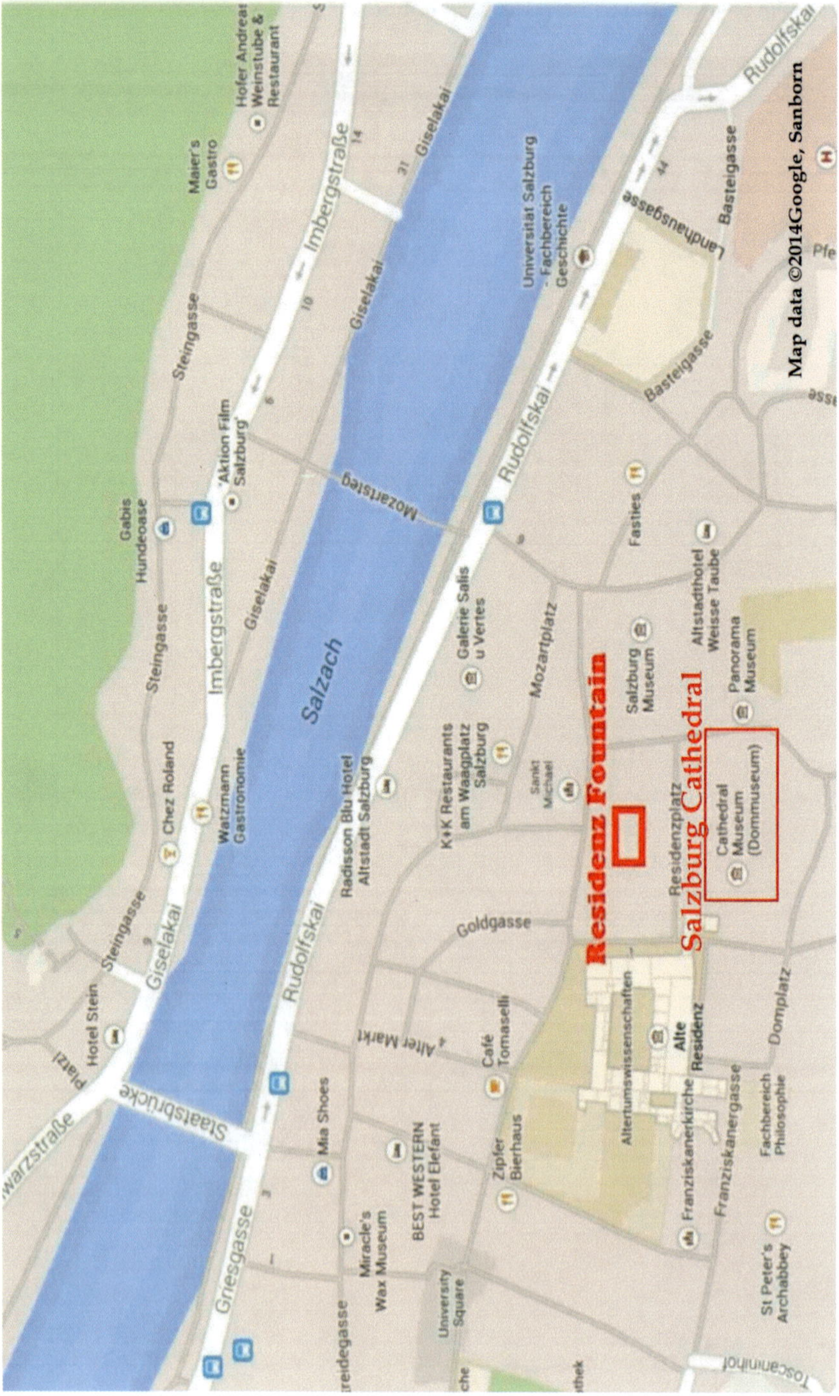

Residenz Fountain
Salzburg Cathedral
Map data ©2014Google, Sanborn
Salzach
Rudolfskai
Giselakai
Imbergstraße
Steingasse
Mozartsteg
Staatsbrücke
Griesgasse
Goldgasse
Mozartplatz
Residenzplatz
Alte Residenz
Domplatz
Cathedral Museum (Dommuseum)
Salzburg Museum
Panorama Museum
Franziskanerkirche
Franziskanergasse
St Peter's Archabbey
Café Tomaselli
Alter Markt
Universität Salzburg - Fachbereich Geschichte
Basteigasse

Residence Fountain in Residence Square

Residence Square is a tourist favourite in Salzburg, it is magnificent and the richly decorated baroque Residence Fountain is the jewel in the crown. Its backdrop is the majestic Salzburg Cathedral and the Old Residence, the palace of the archbishops.

Prince Archbishop Wolf Dietrich tore down over fifty medieval buildings to make room for the building of this square which dates back to 1587. Its fountain was commissioned by Archbishop Guidobald Thun and was designed and sculptured by the Italian sculptor Tommaso di Garone.

Using marble from Mount Untersberg, the fountain was built between 1656- 1661, and is the largest baroque fountain outside of Italy.

The four spouting sea horses guard a rock of sea creatures and animals on which stand four strong men who hold up a large bowl, above which are three dolphins who carry another bowl where Triton holds a snail's shell spouting water skywards.

Horse and Carriage Tour

The Residence Square is also the place where you can go for a tour of Salzburg in a horse's carriage.

You will find your waiting carriage just next to The Salzburg Cathedral almost like a horse taxi rank.

Residence Palace and Salzburg Museum

The old Residential Palace (above) was the Prince Archbishop's place of residence and where important decisions were made regarding their city up to the 19th century. It has over 180 rooms and three large courtyards. It is now open to the public where they can explore the grand staterooms, and is also still used for official receptions and international conferences. Mozart is known to have played in this palace from the age of six. The magnificent staterooms inside are still used today for evening concerts.

Opposite the Old Residence is the **New Residential Palace**, (below) which was built by the bishop for his new residence, but decided against using it as such. Today the palace houses the **Salzburg Museum** which won the European Museum of the year award in 2009.

Mozart's Birthplace

Mozart was born on 27th January 1756 in Getreidegasse 9 in Salzburg. This building is now a museum where you can explore the rooms and artefacts relating to the famous composer.

The displays cover three floors and include the original musical instruments used by Mozart, and displays portraying his family and his later career as a musician and composer. Among the exhibits are the violin he played as a child and the famous clavichord from which he composed 'The Magic Flute'. There are also some very interesting documents written in Mozart's own hand, including a love letter to his wife Constanze.

To visit the other Mozart's Residence you will need to take a short walk across the river, to Mozart Wohnhaus at 8 Markatplatz. This museum also has artefacts including musical instruments paintings and documents, but it's smaller than the Birthplace Museum.

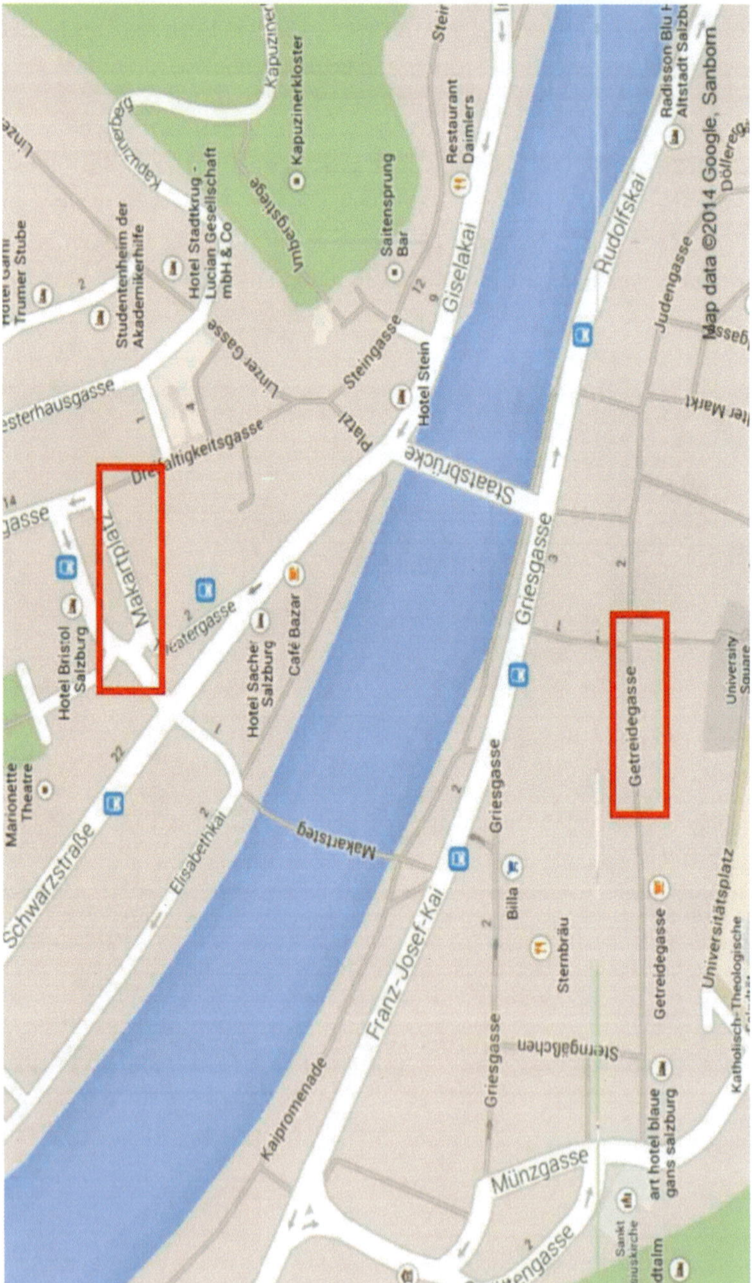
Makartplatz
Getreidegasse
Staatsbrücke
Griesgasse
Rudolfskai
Giselakai
Schwarzstraße
Elisabethkai
Makartsteg
Franz-Josef-Kai
Kaipromenade
Münzgasse
Gstättengasse
Hotel Bristol Salzburg
Hotel Sacher Salzburg
Café Bazar
Marionette Theatre
Hotel Stein
Steingasse
Linzer Gasse
Dreifaltigkeitsgasse
Theatergasse
Kapuzinerkloster
Kapuzinerberg
Hotel Stadtkrug - Lucian Gesellschaft mbH & Co
Studentenheim der Akademikerhilfe
Trumer Stube
Saitensprung Bar
Restaurant Daimlers
Judengasse
Billa
Sternbräu
Sterngäßchen
Universitätsplatz
University Square
art hotel blaue gans salzburg
Map data ©2014 Google, Sanborn

Gertreidgasse

Gertreidgasse

This famous narrow street has charm due to the overhanging intricate gilt and wrought – iron signs that once identified the guilds of the craftsmen who once traded there. The buildings date from the 13th to the 16th century, and of course at number 9 is Mozart's Birthplace. There are many expensive designer shops in this street. Not to be confused with Griesgasse which is a parallel street. The McDonalds is slightly more up market than the ones in the UK. and are on a par with Starbucks, and it has a much more interesting menu than the McDonalds in the UK. It even has its own wrought iron sign.

Mirabell Palace

Mirabell Palace dates back to 1606 and its gardens are a lovely place to roam and relax away from the hustle and bustle of the city. The Palace is a beautiful example of Baroque architecture. The palace was damaged by fire in 1818 and needed to be rebuilt. Unfortunately it is not fully open to the public as it now houses the Mayor's offices and the Municipal Council. The Marble Hall though, a concert hall that was used by Mozart in the past, and still used for concerts today, is free to visit but only at set times, currently Mon, Wed, Thu: 8 am - 4 pm, Tues + Fri: 1 - 4 pm.

Mirabell Gardens

The gardens were designed by the famous architect Fischer Von Erlach in the 18th century. The Pegasus Fountain sculptured by Kaspar Gras was added to the garden in 1913. Not only will visitors enjoy the gardens horticultural beauty, but they will marvel at the view of the fort from its vantage point. The gardens are also very popular with 'The Sound of Music' fans as it was used for the location of the filming of the 'Do- re- mi' song.

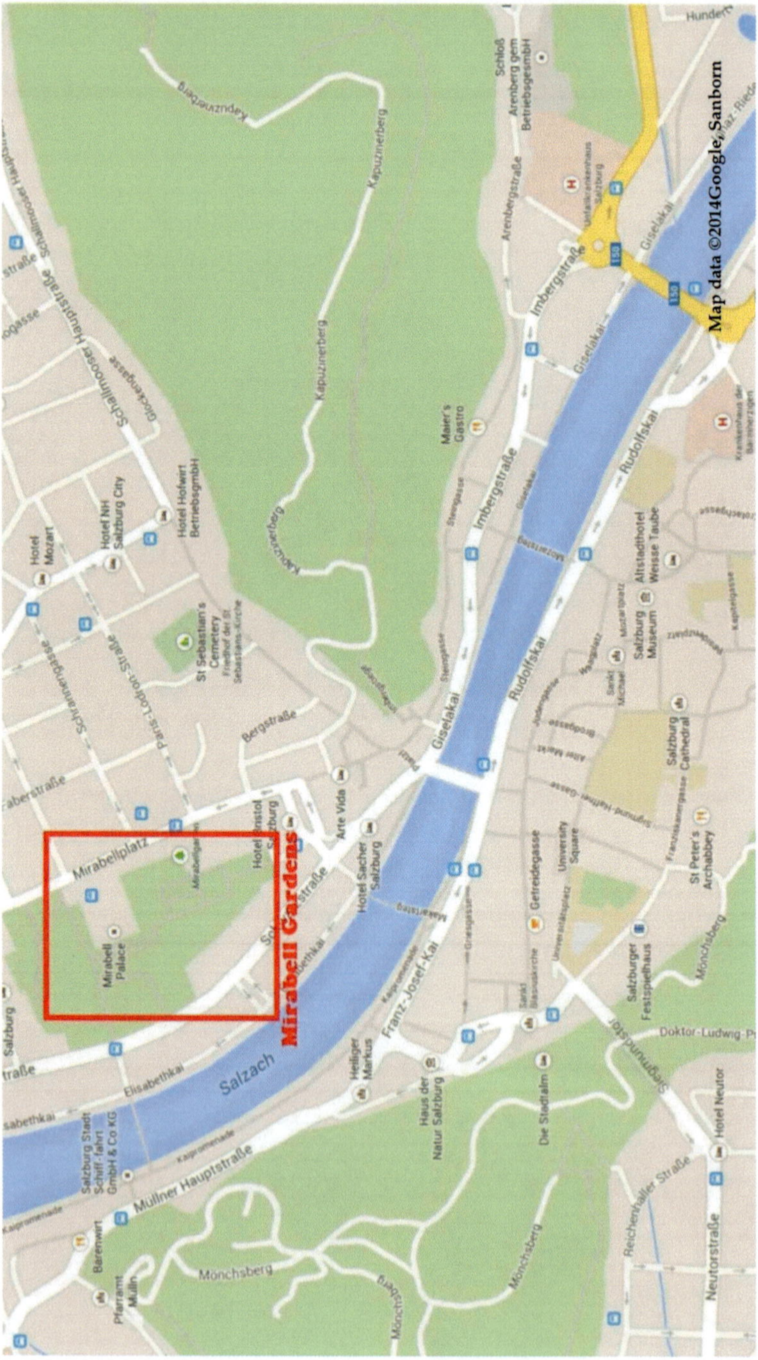
Mirabell Gardens
Map data ©2014Google, Sanborn
Mirabellplatz
Mirabell Palace
Salzach
Elisabethkai
Giselakai
Rudolfskai
Franz-Josef-Kai
Imbergstraße
Kapuzinerberg
Mönchsberg
Müllner Hauptstraße
Salzburg Cathedral
Salzburg Museum
St Peter's Archabbey
Salzburger Festspielhaus
University Square
Getreidegasse
Hotel Sacher Salzburg
St Sebastian's Cemetery
Bergstraße
Paris-Lodron-Straße
Schallmooser Hauptstraße
Hotel Mozart
Hotel NH Salzburg City
Haus der Natur Salzburg
Die Stadtalm
Neutorstraße
Reichenhaller Straße
Siegmundstor
Hotel Neutor
Doktor-Ludwig-Pr
Arte Vida
Maier's Gastro
Altstadthotel Weisse Taube
Heiliger Markus
Bärenwirt
Pfarramt Mülln
Salzburg Stadt Schiff-Fahrt GmbH & Co KG
Arenbergstraße
Hotel Hofwirt BetriebsgmbH

Nonnberg Abbey

Nonnberg convent was founded by St Rupert, who was the Bishop of Worms in Germany in the year 700 AD.

The Abbey became famous because of the story of the Von Trapp family and its location being used in the movie 'The Sound of Music'. Maria in the biography, from which the movie was based, was indeed a Nunn at this convent and did indeed marry the Captain after she was hired as the children's governess. The convent had encouraged her to marry the captain, and she spoke about wanting to go back to the Abbey. In real life though she claimed she only married the captain so she could stay with the children whom she had grown fond of. The real life story does have a lot of similarities with the movie, but there are also some differences.

St Rupert's sister Erentrudis was made Abbess of the convent around 715 AD.

The Abbey itself is closed to the public, but visitors can explore the church.

At the back of the church behind glass are some well preserved Romanesque frescos that date back to 1150. (Left) To see them though, you need to put in a coin to switch on the light

Nonnberg Abbey
Map data ©2014Google, Sanborn
Salzach
Karolinen Brücke
Bürglsteinstraße
Hellbrunner Straße
Ignaz-Rieder-Kai
Franz-Hinterholzer-Kai
Giselakai
Rudolfskai
Petersbrunnstraße
Nonntaler Hauptstraße
Nonnberggasse
Erhardgäßchen
Kaigasse
Nonnbergstiege
Festungsgasse
Kapitelplatz
Mozartplatz
Pfeifergasse
Basteigasse
Krotachgasse
Herrengasse
Kapitelgasse
Landesgericht Salzburg
Stift Nonnberg
Pfarramt Nonntal St Erhard
Festung Hohensalzburg
Fortress Hohensalzburg
Salzburg Museum
Panorama Museum
Unipark Nonntal
Borg-Nonntal
Salzburger Kunstverein

St Peters Abbey

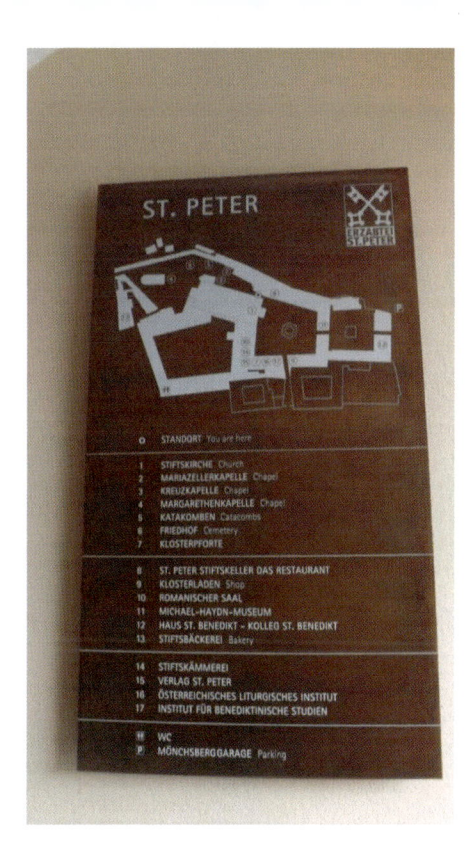

St Peter's Abbey was founded by St Rupert. He had travelled east along the Danube then west at the river Enns until he arrived in a ruined Roman town of Iuvavum. Rupert settled here and founded the building of St Peter's Abbey and also of the nearby Nonnberg Abbey. Iuvavum later became known as Salzburg.

Mozart's famous 'Great Mass' in C Minor was performed here at St Peter's in 1783.

St. Rupert is entombed near the altar. St Vitalis, Mozart's sister Maria, and the composer Johann Michael Haydn are also entombed here.

There is a library at St Peters and is said to hold over 120,000 volumes of manuscripts, deeds, records, photographs and maps, and musical scores, dating from the 8th century until the present day.

The outside graveyards and catacombs are popular with tourists, and were used as a basis for design for 'The Sound of Music' scenes where the Von Trapp family try to escape. These scenes though are thought to have been filmed on a film set in Hollywood.

Many of the graves are those of the Salzburg aristocracy

Above the Catacombs within the cliff wall in St Peters graveyard. There is a fee on entry to the Catacombs.

St Peter's Cemetery.

St Peter's Abbey
St Peter's Archabbey
St. Peter Stiftskeller Das
Salzburg University
Salzburg Museum
Fortress Hohensalzburg
Kaisererbräu
Salzach
Rudolfskai
Giselakai
Griesgasse
Imbergstraße
Getreidegasse
University Square
Felsenreitschule
Haus der Natur Salzburg
Café Bazar
Mönchsberg
Hellbrunner Straße
Franz-Hinterholzer-Kai
Ignaz-Rieder-Kai
Petersbrunnstraße
Salzburger Kunstverein
JUFA Salzburg City
Hotel Star Inn Salzburg Zentrum
Brunnhausgasse
Kapuzinerberg
Doktor-Ludwig-Prähauser-Weg

Makartsteg Bridge

The Makartsteg is the lover's bridge because the railing houses a sea of padlocks expressing love for another, and they are a permanent fixture on the bridge so a memento the couple can share and leave their mark on Salzburg. You can take a lock already prepared with you, or buy one in the gift shops nearby. If you want your lock to be different and stand out it is probably better to take one with you before you go as the ones in the gift shops all look similar. The bridge is the most famous in Salzburg so even if you don't intend on leaving a lock, you can still walk its path taking in the beautiful views of the river Salzach.

Makartsteg
Elisabethkai
Franz-Josef-Kai
Kaipromenade
Griesgasse
Staatsbrücke
Giselakai
Rudolfskai
Makartplatz
Theatergasse
Dreifaltigkeitsgasse
Linzer Gasse
Steingasse
Platzl
Hotel Stein
Hotel Sacher Salzburg
Café Bazar
Hotel Bristol Salzburg
Studentenheim der Akademikerhilfe
Hotel Stadtkrug - Lucian Gesellschaft mbH & Co
Saitensprung Bar
Imbergstiege
Getreidegasse
Sterngäßchen
Sternbräu
Billa
Münzgasse
Gstättengasse
Universitätsplatz
University Square
Katholisch-Theologische Fakultät
Zipfer Bierhaus
Judengasse
art hotel blaue gans salzburg
Die Stadtalm
Sankt Blasiuskirche
Haus der Salzburg
Map data ©2014 Google, Sanborn

Austrian Food

You cannot go to Austria and not sample the Salzburg Nockerlin or their traditional dish of Wiener Schnitzel.

They do beautiful ones here at the café Mozart, which is near to McDonalds on Gertreidegasse.

70

If you like sausages you are in luck, you will find many food vans around like the one above.

You can also find lavish markets such as the one above in Altr Market.

Seafood markets such as the one above should get any fish lover's taste buds tingling.

Above Altr market.

Giselakai
Restaurant Daimlers
Griesgasse
Staatsbrücke
Rudolfskai
Judengasse
Goldgasse
Brodgasse
Alter Markt
Döllerergäßchen
Residenzplatz
Getreidegasse
Universitätsplatz
Radisson Blu Hotel Altstadt Salzburg
O'Malley's
Maredo Steak-Restaurant
Segabar
myindigo Staatsbrücke
Salzburger Sparkasse Bank
Rositta
Café Tomaselli
Surjit Singh Saran
Hotel Zur Goldene Ente
Café-Konditorei Fürst
Hotel Am Dom
Josef Manner & Comp.
Jahn-Markl Leder- u Trachtenbekleidung
Galerie Welz
Zipfer Bierhaus
dm drogerie markt
Mia Shoes
Miracle's Wax Museum
Schatz-Konditorei
Tea & Co. Handels GmbH
'Zum Eulenspiegel' Hotel- und Restaurant-Betriebsgesellschaft mbH
Burger King
Mozart-Museum (Mozarts Geburtshaus) und Mozart-Archiv
Hagenauerstuben
University Square
Espresso Fabrizi
University of Salzburg Church
Artmosphere Galerien GmbH Rudolf Budja Galerie
KA-International Eybl GmbH & Co.KG
Triangel
K+K Restaurant am Waagplatz Salzburg
Sankt Michael
Map data ©2014 Google, Sanborn

For an evening out, particularly if you like opera or 'The Sound of Music', I can recommend you go for an evening meal at 'The Sound of Salzburg Show'. It is a small venue, of less than 100 people. They serve you dinner an hour before the show, then entertain you with opera and The Sound of Music songs.

You can find out more about the evening here http://www.soundofsalzburg.info/

There is also a popular Mozart Dinner can you can go to, in the oldest restaurant in Salzburg, attached to St Peter's where you will be entertained with live opera while you dine.

Shopping

There is no shortage of Spar shops in Salzburg, ranging from small corner shops to large supermarkets. Here you will find cheaper drinks and snacks if you are on a budget or want something to take back to your hotel.

The chocolate shops such as the one above are everywhere. Mozartkugel are spherical chocolate balls which are filled with pistachio marzipan, nougat and chocolate. They have novelty gifts boxes such as violin shaped boxes, and can be expensive in the speciality shops and gift shops, but you will probably find them at a cheaper price in Spar.

There are a lot of different speciality types of shops that you may find interesting, such as this traditional costume shop above.

The Lakes and Mountains

Salzburg is nestled very near the majestic mountains and the beautiful Lake District.

You can visit the lakes via the same company that does 'The Sound of Music Tour' you can book in advance at www.salzburg-sightseeingtours.at

A courier will pick you up from your hotel and ferry you to the bus terminal near Mirabell Gardens. After a short ride you are dropped off at St Gilgen, where you will pick up the ferry for a fifty minute journey on course for St Wolfgang across the lake of Wolfgangsee pictured above.

The ferry has a cafe inside where you can buy drinks and snacks. The journey to St Wolfgang across the tranquil crystal waters is breathtaking.

On arrival to St Wolfgang you will be free to explore the historic village at your leisure.

The village has a charm all of its own. Every building has its own unique character, the central feature being the Pfarrkirche St. Wolfgang (Pilgrimage Church of St. Wolfgang)

The church is close to the lake and gives picturesque views.

It's a paradise location for photographers as there is beauty around every corner.

St Wolfgang has many interesting historic buildings such as the ones above. Its cobbled streets are laden with small outdoor cafes and small gift shops to explore.

It is a very worthwhile trip if you have the time. Highly recommended.

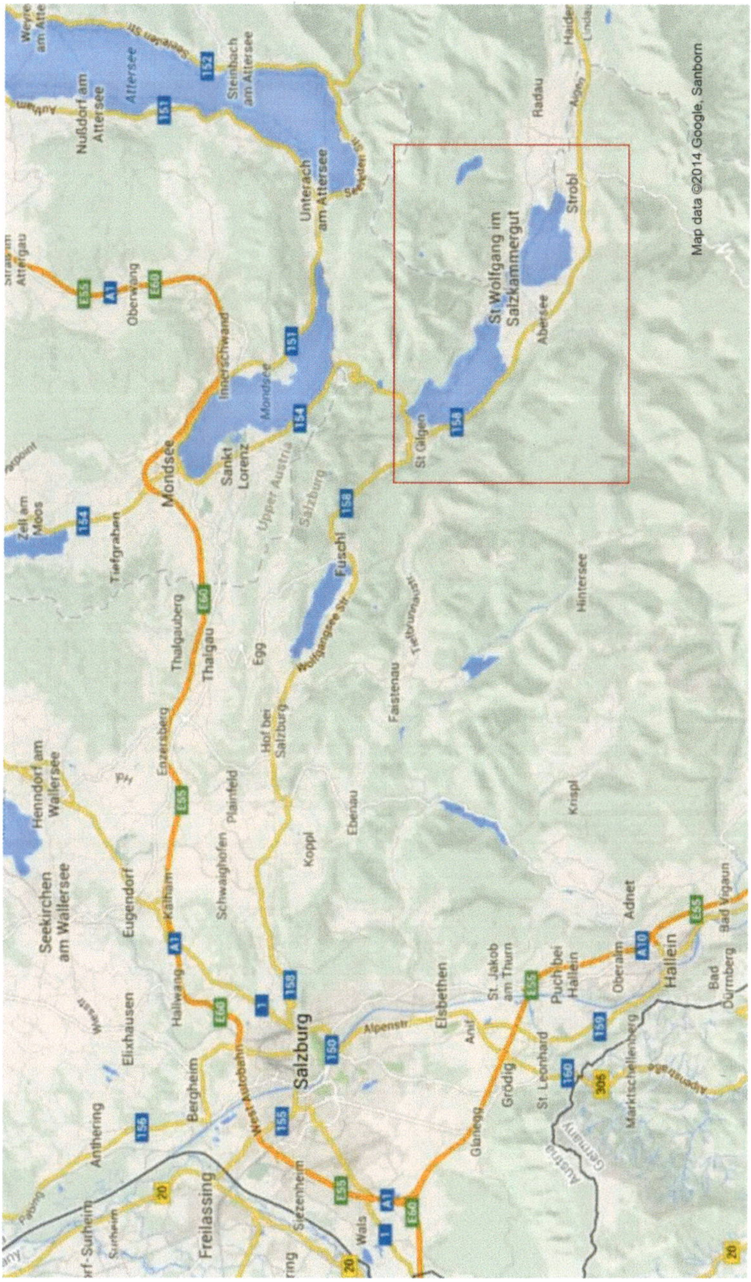
Salzburg
Freilassing
Seekirchen am Wallersee
Henndorf am Wallersee
Eugendorf
Elixhausen
Bergheim
Anthering
Hallwang
Kalham
Schwaighofen
Plainfeld
Koppl
Ebenau
Hof bei Salzburg
Thalgau
Thalgauberg
Enzersberg
Egg
Fuschl
Faistenau
Hintersee
Krispl
Adnet
Hallein
Bad Dürrnberg
Bad Vigaun
Oberalm
Puch bei Hallein
St. Jakob am Thurn
Elsbethen
Anif
Grödig
St. Leonhard
Glanegg
Marktschellenberg
Wals
Siezenheim
Mondsee
Sankt Lorenz
Innerschwand
Oberwang
Tiefgraben
Zell am Moos
St Gilgen
St Wolfgang im Salzkammergut
Abersee
Strobl
Radau
Unterach am Attersee
Nußdorf am Attersee
Steinbach am Attersee
Attersee
Mondsee
Upper Austria
Salzburg
Austria
Germany
West Autobahn
Alpenstr
Wolfgangsee Str
Map data ©2014 Google, Sanborn

Hellbrunn Palace

If you visited the Gazebo here on the Sound of Music Tour it is worth another visit. It is accessible via the 25 bus route from Mirabell Platz, and just 7 Km outside of Salzburg.
http://www.salzburg-ag.at/fileadmin/user_upload/content/download/Linie_25_2013.pdf

Initially a country residence built in 1612 at the foot of Hellbrunn Mountain, commissioned by the Archbishop Markus Sittikus von Hohenems. Markus Sittikus must have had a great sense of humour as he designed trick fountains. One trick was, as the Archbishop was seated at the table in the garden with his guests, a fountain could be started which would soak the guest from underneath the seats but leave the Bishop clean and dry. Other fountains in the water themed gardens also surprise the guests. I don't want to spoil all of the surprises, but if you do go, plan to get wet.

The visit will be thoroughly entertaining, particularly for children. The zoo is not far from here.

And if you didn't get to go on The Sound of Music Tour, the Gazebo is worth a visit too.

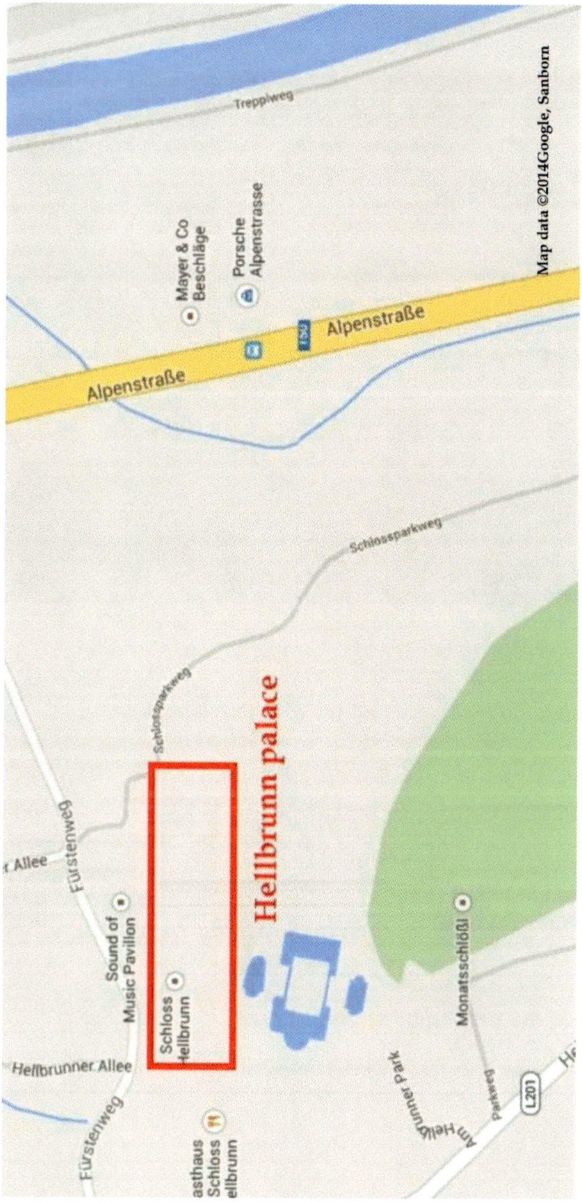
Hellbrunn palace
Map data ©2014Google, Sanborn
Treppiweg
Mayer & Co Beschläge
Porsche Alpenstrasse
Alpenstraße
Alpenstraße
Schlossparkweg
Schlossparkweg
Fürstenweg
Sound of Music Pavillon
Schloss Hellbrunn
Hellbrunner Allee
Fürstenweg
Monatsschlößl
Hellbrunner Park
Parkweg
L201

Winter in Salzburg

Thousand flock to Salzburg in winter as it turns into a winter wonderland.

The Christmas Markets are a big attraction between late November and the end of December.

Where Cathedral Square transforms into an enchanted Christmas Village, where market stalls are laden with homemade foods and handicrafts, gifts and ornaments. Catering to all of your senses, feasting your eyes on the colourful gifts, as you take in the aroma of the gingerbread, roast chestnuts and mulled wine, while you listen to the heavenly Salzburg Choirs.

Find out more about the Christmas Markets here-

http://www.austria.info/uk/winter-holidays-austria/christmas-markets-in-salzburg-1428444.html

Skiing brings tens of thousands of visitors to the Alps every year. The skiing season varies but is typically at its peak between late December and Early March.

Salzburg's biggest skiing resort is Ski Amade, with 270 lifts and 860 kilometres of slopes its claimed to be the biggest ski resort in Europe. http://www.visit-salzburg.net/travel/ski-amade.htm

More about skiing in Austria here- http://www.visit-salzburg.net/travel/skiing-austria.htm

Other Attractions to Visit.

The Salzburg Zoo.

The Salzburg Zoo is south of Salzburg more details here -
http://www.salzburg.info/en/sights/excursions/salzburg_zoo

There is a bus that goes there, the number 25 from Mirabell Platz.

http://www.salzburg-ag.at/fileadmin/user_upload/content/download/Linie_25_2013.pdf

The Salt Mines
http://www.salzburg.info/en/sights/excursions/salt_mines_in_hallein

The sightseeing tour provides a day at the salt mines.

http://www.salzburg-sightseeingtours.at/rundfahrten_detail.php?tourid=81&lang=1

Vienna

Vienna is almost a 3 hour drive if you hire a car or a 2 and a half hour train ride. It's about a 20 minute walk from Mirabell Platz, but there are buses that go from there.

Keltenblitz

Toboggan runs from the top of the mountain Zinkenkogel in Hallein Bad Duerrnberg. There is a chair lift to take you to the top of the mountain, and suitable for all ages, is the Toboggan ride that will carry you 2,200 metres to the valley below.

Just a few Km from Salzburg, you can find more details here.

http://www.tennengau.com/
http://www.duerrnberg.at/index.php?option=com_content&view=article&id=57&Itemid=59

Video
http://www.duerrnberg.at/index.php?option=com_content&view=article&id=69&Itemid=74

Addresses of Attractions

Cafe Mozart
Getreidegasse 22
5020 Salzburg
+43.662.843958

Felsenreitschule (Rock Riding School)
Hoffstallgasse 1
520 Salzburg
+43.662.849097

Festungsbahn
Festungsgasse 4
5020 Salzburg
+43 662 8884-9750

Frohnburg
Hellbrunner Allee 53
5020 Salzburg
+43.662.6208260

Hellbrunn Palace
Furstenweg 37
5020 Salzburg
+43.662.820372

Hohensalzburg Fortress
Monchsberg 34
5020 Salzburg
+43.662.842411

Keltenblitz
A-5422 Bad Duerrenberg
Weissenwaschweg 19
+43.6245.85105

Mirabell Palace and Gardens
Mirabell Platz 4
5020 Salzburg
+43.662.80720

Mondsee Abbey
Kirchengasse 1
Mondsee
Oberosterreich A
5310

Mozart Geburtshaus (Birthplace)
Getreidegasse 9
5020 Salzburg
+43.662.844313

Mozart Dinner
St Peter Stiftskeller-Das Restaurant
St Peter Bezirk 1/4
5020 Salzburg
+43 662 8412680
http://www.stpeter-stiftskeller.at/index.php

Mozart's Residence
Makartplatz 8
5020 Salzburg
+43.662.874227-40

Nonnberg Abbey
Nonnberggasse 2
5020 Salzburg
+43.662.841607

Pferdeschwemme (Horse Well)
Herbert Von Karajanplatz
5020 Salzburg

Salzburg Cathedral
Domplatz 1a
5020 Salzburg
+43.662.8047-7950

Salzburg Museum
Neue Residenz, Mozartplatz 1
5020 Salzburg
+43.662.620808-700

Salzburg Zoo
Anifer Landessstrabe 1
5081 Anif
+43.662.8201760

Schloss Leopoldskron

Leopoldskrontrable 56-58

5020 Salzburg

+43.662.839830

Sound of Salzburg Show

K+K restaurants

am Waagplatz 2

5020 Salzburg

+43.662.23105800

www.soundofsalzburg.info/online-booking

Sound of Music Bus Tour

Mirabell Platz 2

5020 Salzburg.

+43.662.881616

www.salzburg-sightseeingtours.at

St Peter's Abbey

 St. Peter Bezirk 1,

Postfach 113,

5010 Salzburg

+43.662.844576

Wolfgangsee Boats
Markt 35
5360 St. Wolfgang
+43.6138.2232
http://www.schafbergbahn.at/de_at/ueber-die-schifffahrt/flotte.html

http://www.schafbergbahn.at/content/dam/websites/schafbergbahn/Folder/Saisoneroeffnung2014.pdf

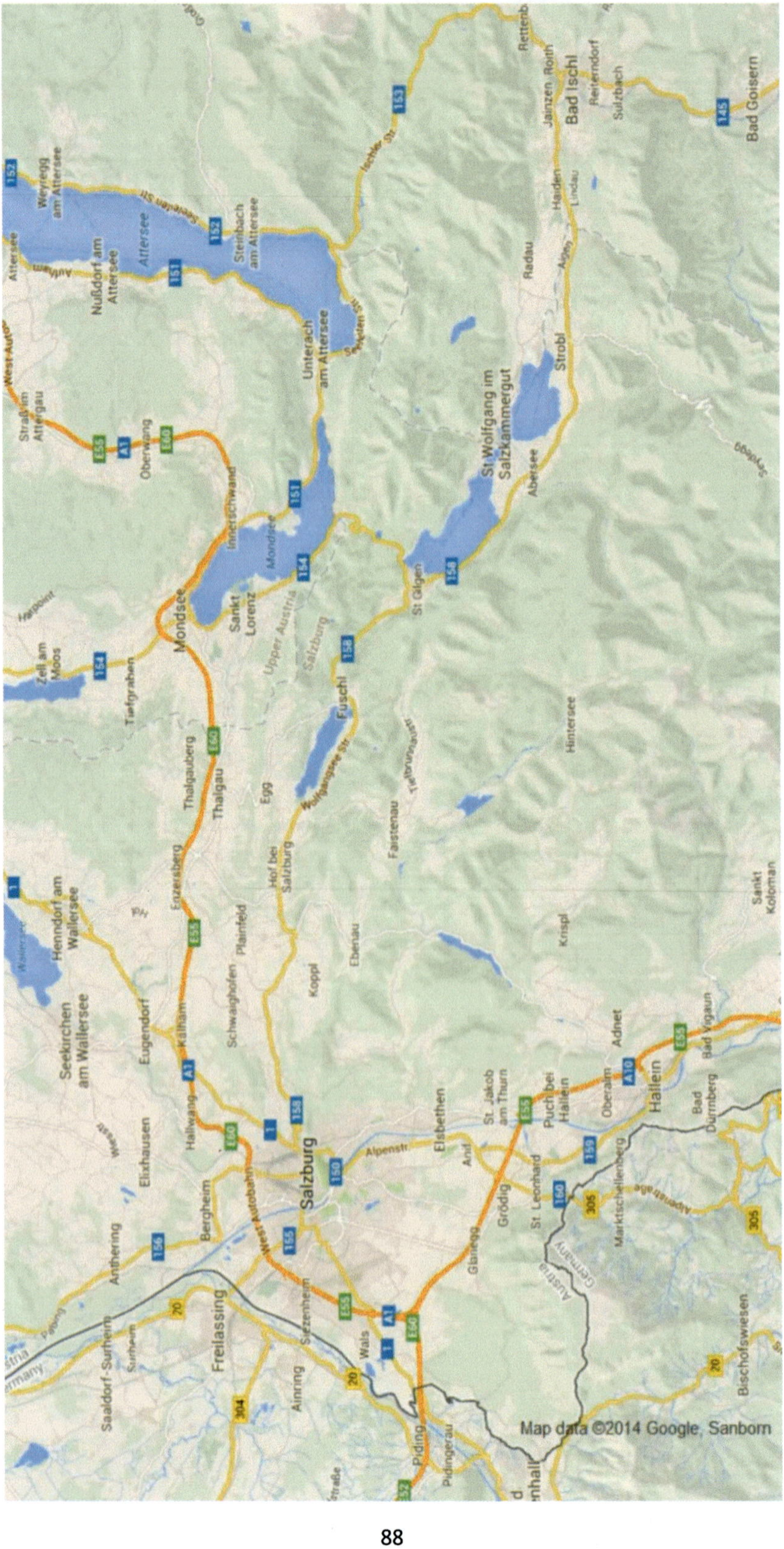
Attersee
Nußdorf am Attersee
Steinbach am Attersee
Weyregg am Attersee
Unterach am Attersee
Straß im Attergau
Oberwang
Innerschwand
Mondsee
Sankt Lorenz
Zell am Moos
Tiefgraben
Thalgauberg
Thalgau
Egg
Fuschl
Upper Austria
Salzburg
Wolfgangsee Str.
Ischler Str.
Bad Ischl
Jainzen
Rettenb
Reiterndorf
Sulzbach
Bad Goisern
Haiden
Lindau
Radau
Strobl
St Wolfgang im Salzkammergut
Abersee
St Gilgen
Faistenau
Hintersee
Hof bei Salzburg
Plainfeld
Enzersberg
Henndorf am Wallersee
Seekirchen am Wallersee
Eugendorf
Kalham
Schwaighofen
Koppl
Ebenau
Krispl
Sankt Koloman
Hallwang
Elixhausen
Anthering
Bergheim
Salzburg
Alpenstr.
Elsbethen
Anif
Grödig
St. Leonhard
St. Jakob am Thurn
Puch bei Hallein
Oberalm
Adnet
Hallein
Bad Vigaun
Bad Dürrnberg
Marktschellenberg
Freilassing
Saaldorf-Surheim
Siezenheim
Wals
Ainring
Piding
Bischofswiesen
Glanegg
West Autobahn
Austria
Germany
Map data ©2014 Google, Sanborn

Copyright 2014 by Sarah Lee

All rights reserved. No part of this publication may be reproduced, distributed, or transmitted in any form or by any means, including photocopying, recording, or other electronic or mechanical methods, without the prior written permission of the publisher.

The author has worked hard to authenticate the reliability of this travel guide, however liability cannot be accepted for its accuracy.

Mondsee Cathedral.

Printed in Great Britain
by Amazon.co.uk, Ltd.,
Marston Gate.